blackjack's
HIDDEN SECRETS
Win Without Counting

by GEORGE PAPPADOPOULOS

Blackjack's Hidden Secrets, Win Without Counting
George Pappadopoulos

ME-n-U Marketers
POB 127
Linwood, NJ 08221
Fax: 609-653-8186
Email: MEnUMark@aol.com

Find us on the World Wide Web at: http://www.blackjacknocounting.com

Cover and Book Design: Rose De Dan, Cat Dancing Design
Editor: Francine G. De Dan
Printer: Quick Stop Printing

Pappadopoulos, George.
    Blackjack's hidden secrets : win without
counting / by George Pappadopoulos. -- 2nd ed.
        p. cm.
    ISBN: 0-9673795-1-2

    1. Blackjack (Game)   I. Title.

    GV1295.B55P37 2000   795.4'23
                    QBI00-500131

New and expanded edition, 1999
First printing 12/99
Second Printing 3/00
Third Printing 5/00
Fourth Printing 10/00
Fifth Printing 12/01

Printed and bound in the United States of America.

/ // /// //// *TABLE OF CONTENTS*

/ // /// //// *ACKNOWLEDGMENTS*

At this time I would like to thank all those who have contributed to my knowledge. This book could not have been written nor my system developed without the pioneering perseverance of these gifted men. Among them are: Dr. Edward Thorpe, Ken Uston, Lawrence Revere, Julian Braun, Stanford Wong, Bobby Singer, Arnold Snyder, Jerry Patterson, Peter Griffin, Donald Schlesinger and a special thanks to John Patrick.

Francine De Dan, thank you for being my partner. Without you this book would only be a dream. You and you alone have been the emotional force that has inspired me to write this book. Your countless hours of dedication coupled with your unwavering confidence in me has transformed a difficult task into a simple pleasure. Anyone can have a partner but not everyone can have a true friend. I have both.

Rose De Dan, thank you for your unique ability to formulate my written thoughts into a book that can be read by many and understood by all.

Mrs. D., thank you for being there in the wee hours of the morning when no one else could possibly have functioned much less cared.

Scott Peterson, thank you for being my Internet mentor. I consider myself fortunate to have a guide like you in cyberspace.

Steve Weinman, thank you for being there when the cry for help came through.

John Pappadopoulos, thank you for being the kind of brother everyone wants but very few have.

Chris Jackson, thank you for your time and effort in showing me how the same thoughts can be expressed in different ways.

My name is George Pappadopoulos and I have been a consistent winner in blackjack with a win percentage of 78%. I began playing over five years ago because I had a lot of time on my hands and needed a challenge. For 21 years I had owned a very successful restaurant, but divorce forced me to sell. Moving to Atlantic City, I went to work for a major casino. Since food and beverage was my expertise I obtained a position in the food and beverage department. After two years I became complacent and began searching for something that would challenge my mind. I decided on blackjack. I thought that beating the casino at their own game would give me the challenge I was seeking and I couldn't have been more correct. The high I received by beating them was greater than I expected.

Bear in mind I am no rocket scientist or Harvard graduate. In fact, I never went to college nor do I possess a genius IQ. I'm just an average person, looking to create a way of beating the house consistently in an uncomplicated fashion, unlike card counting. According to all the experts, card counting is the only way to beat the casinos. I emphatically disagree with this theory and can prove it. When I began I did not want to put in the tremendous amount of time and effort it takes to learn card counting. Don't let anyone tell you differently, it literally takes hundreds of hours and a huge bankroll to learn to count cards accurately. I'm going to teach you how to be a consistent winner within two hours, yes, I said TWO hours maximum, without reading books, going to blackjack schools, etc.

Some of the most complicated problems in the world are resolved with simple, logical solutions and that's basically what I am going to teach you. I am now going to use the word theory, which I will make reference to many times throughout this text, because until you begin winning consistently it can only be a theory. I have used this formula thousands of times and have consistently won 78%* of the time, therefore for me this formula is not a theory it is a fact. The experts will tell you that you can only win consistently if you're a card counter. To them I say use my theory and you'll never count cards again.

You might ask yourself, "How did I come up with this theory?" It wasn't easy—I went to the largest gambling bookstore in the area and bought every book on blackjack I could find by all the leading experts in the field. I then proceeded to read all of them from cover to cover several times. This task was quite involved and took many hours to complete. Through my reading, I found that no two experts agree—that each has their own theory, and each believes theirs to be correct. I did discover that much of what each said was true, but for me, they all rely too heavily on card counting. Like a jig saw puzzle, the problem was getting all of their good ideas to fit together—formulating a system that a normal, everyday person, like me, could win consistently with, without counting cards. It took a number of years of trial and error to come up with my winning formula, but my efforts have not been in vain.

Not only does my theory work, when I play I am not persecuted by the casinos, as card counters are.

*Individual results may vary depending on accuracy in following the system.

In fact, I am given unlimited comps on a regular basis just so they can get my action. I'm talking about gourmet restaurants, beautiful rooms, headliner shows, etc. If I were to be labeled a card counter they would not give me the time of day. Known card counters are banned from every casino in the world except New Jersey. In New Jersey, specifically Atlantic City, it is against the law to ban a card counter from playing. This law came into effect in 1984 when a decision from the state supreme court declared it discriminatory and unconstitutional. The casinos fight back once they suspect you are a card counter—and the key word is suspect—they don't have to prove it. They discourage you from playing by reshuffling the shoe after every hand. They are allowed to do this by law, which gives you no chance to count cards and neutralizes whichever card counting system you are using, making card counting a worthless skill. So why spend the tremendous amount of time and effort learning something you can't use? The experts do not address this problem. They are only interested in selling you a book whether you can use most of the material written in it or not, because 80% of every book I've read is about card counting and card counting systems.

With extensive research into formulating my theory, and thousands of hours of play in numerous casinos, I have consistently beaten the casinos at their own game. I'm now going to show you how to accomplish this in less than two hours of study. I realize this is an incredible statement, however, as I have stated before, some of the most complicated problems require the simplest of solutions. I do not believe in luck, I believe in knowledge. Within the scope of this book I will provide you with the knowledge I have gained from my in-depth study of the game of blackjack.

If my formula were a menu, you would have just completed the appetizer. Now it's time to get into the main course, the meat and potatoes of my formula, and later, when you leave the table, you'll be able to enjoy the sweetest of desserts—your pockets will be filled with the kind of excitement you can spend in a supermarket, put in the bank, or just give away, the choice is yours.

There are five rules you must learn in order to become successful with my theory. I cannot stress enough how important it is to learn all five—not four out of five, or three out of five—but all five. If you can't do that you may as well stop reading and go have a hamburger because you won't be eating a sirloin steak unless you follow my formula exactly, to the letter. On this I must insist—I'm not being difficult, but we are talking about your money!

If, after reading this book, you have questions, stories or feedback, you may contact me, George Pappadopoulos, at MEnUMark@aol.com or POB 127, Linwood, NJ 08221.

Without the proper bankroll you should not be in a casino. You would have a better chance of winning by buying lottery tickets. So you ask yourself, "What is the proper bankroll?" The answer is 40 times the table minimum. Examples are: if you play at a $5 table you need $200, $10 table you need $400, $25 table you need $1000, and $100 table you need $4000. You must have this money available before you enter the casino and only, I repeat, only that amount, no more no less. I cannot emphasize enough how important this is.

Now let's talk about win goals and loss limits. Your bankroll determines both. My theory eliminates all the guess work in your decision. For example: if you are playing at a $5 table you must bring $200, therefore your loss limit is $200 maximum. Remember, if you lose you do not take any other money from any other source to continue playing. This means no ATM, no credit card withdrawals and no borrowing money from a friend. If you lose your $200 you are done for the day. You must accept the fact that you cannot win 100% of the time, no one can! On the other hand, if you are playing at a $5 table and you win $100 you are also done for the day. You have achieved your maximum win goal (which is 50% of your bankroll)—go home, you have accomplished what you set out to do—WIN! Remember, I said this is your MAXIMUM LOSS limit and MAXIMUM WIN goal. If you are happy winning $50, go home, there is certainly no shame leaving the casino a winner, on the contrary, you have just beaten them at their own game and you deserve a pat on the back as you walk out the front door. Conversely, if you lose $100 and you feel it's just not your day, go home. The casinos are open 24 hours a day, 7 days a week and they will be there long after you and I are gone.

Now, I'm going to tell you something no other gambler will tell you, it's something I do and I don't know of anyone else who does. If I reach my maximum win goal and the table is red hot—I still go home—I've just accomplished something that no other investment can do, I have increased my bankroll by 50% in only a few hours of work. Show me another investment that can do this consistently and I'll consider changing my philosophy. This is one of many reasons that I am a consistent winner. Surveys have shown that 75% of all casino players are winning at one time or another during their visit, however less than 4% go home winners, and less than 1/10 of 1% win consistently. Can you guess the reason why? They get greedy. Remember—you cannot break the casino, they have too much money. It's better to have a piece of the pie than none at all. Learn how to win.

In all the books I've read, basic strategy is the only guideline consistently agreed upon. Basic strategy has been proven to be mathematically correct, just like 1+1=2 and 2+2=4. The basic strategy chart I will give you will be your bible. It is accepted and practiced by every professional blackjack player I know and is contained in every blackjack book I have read, regardless of their other opinions and disagreements, of which there are many. This basic strategy chart was comprised by putting 10 billion—yes, I said 10 billion—hands of blackjack into a computer, and computing the best percentage of each hand's outcome. This is not an opinion or a theory, it is a mathematical fact. Once you memorize this basic strategy chart you have the foundation for becoming a consistent winner. Knowing this information makes the difference between being an investor or just being a player. Remember there are many players but very few investors. Which do you want to be?

The basic strategy chart does not give you guarantees, it gives you winning percentages. For example: if the dealer has a picture as his up card and you have a hard 16—meaning you must hit until you reach a hard 17—you will break 70% of the time, losing that hand. However, if you choose to stand you will lose 76% of the time. This is a mathematical fact based on the 10 billion computerized hands of blackjack. I could go on and on with different percentages, but why bore you. Trust me, the results are factual not theoretical.

Before showing you the basic strategy chart I would like to mention a few situations you might encounter at a table.

Never, ever, listen to anyone at a table regarding what you should or should not do. Remember, 99% of the people you are playing with do not know basic strategy perfectly. You are not allowed to make even one mistake, it will cost you, and could be the difference between walking out a winner or loser. Don't ever trust a dealer, he or she would not intentionally tell you something wrong, however they are far from perfect themselves. Now and then you may come across someone at your table who does not understand basic strategy and says something like "if you hadn't hit that hand the dealer would have broken,"—ignore them. In a short period of time he or she will probably leave and go bother someone else.

Bear in mind that whatever others do will not affect your play as long as you are perfect with your basic strategy. This is also a proven fact. The only effect it might have on you is psychological. For example, if someone has two 10 value cards and decides to split them and this bothers you, leave the table and find another one you are comfortable with. Personally, I don't care what anyone does at the table, I follow what I know is correct—if they want to lose their money let them. Blackjack is not a game of hunches, whims or feelings, it is simply mathematical. Play with your head, not your heart.

Try not to have any conversation with the dealer or others at your table. You must focus and concentrate on your objective—winning. I don't know how many times I've heard people say, "I'm just here to have fun"—if that's what you want then this book is not for you, I'm here to teach you how to win. I personally can't see how losing your hard-earned money can be fun. My idea of fun is leaving the table with the casino's money.

These are only a few examples of how people lose consistently. There are many more but I do not want to waste your time reading, nor my time writing, about losers. I'm here to teach you how to win consistently. That's where I'd like to focus our energy and thoughts.

Now, let me explain the difference between hard and soft hands. A soft hand is one in which the Ace can be counted as a one or an eleven. For example: Ace, 9; Ace, 2; Ace, 4, 4; Ace, 6 are all soft hands. You cannot break by hitting a soft hand, which means that the next card cannot put you over 21. In hard hands an ace can only be counted as one, for example: Ace, 5, 6; Ace, 7, 10; Ace, 3, 8. It also means that the next card could put you over 21.

The basic strategy chart I am now going to show you must be known perfectly before you enter the casino. This is the bible, please be aware that I did not invent this card. It is basic strategy agreed upon by every expert in the field. It is what 10 billion hands of blackjack put into a computer produce as your best winning percentage. This is not theoretical, it is mathematical fact. So if someone tells you it's wrong don't waste your breath answering him/her, they obviously don't have a clue about basic strategy.

BASIC STRATEGY CHART

HIT = ☐   STAND = S   DOUBLE = D   SPLIT = X

YOUR HAND	DEALER'S UP CARD									
	2	3	4	5	6	7	8	9	10	A
8										
9		D	D	D	D					
10	D	D	D	D	D	D	D	D		
11	D	D	D	D	D	D	D	D	D	
12			S	S	S					
13	S	S	S	S	S					
14	S	S	S	S	S					
15	S	S	S	S	S					
16	S	S	S	S	S					
A-2				D	D					
A-3				D	D					
A-4			D	D	D					
A-5			D	D	D					
A-6		D	D	D	D					
A-7	S	D	D	D	D	S	S			
A-8	S	S	S	S	S	S	S	S	S	S
A-9	S	S	S	S	S	S	S	S	S	S
A-A	X	X	X	X	X	X	X	X	X	X
2-2	X	X	X	X	X	X				
3-3	X	X	X	X	X	X				
4-4				X	X					
5-5	D	D	D	D	D	D	D	D		
6-6	X	X	X	X	X					
7-7	X	X	X	X	X	X				
8-8	X	X	X	X	X	X	X	X	X	X
9-9	X	X	X	X	X	S	X	X	S	S
YOUR HAND	2	3	4	5	6	7	8	9	10	A
	DEALER'S UP CARD									

Two more mathematical rules are:
1. Never, ever, take insurance even when you have blackjack;
2. Always split Ace's and 8's.

You must accept them as law, they are mathematically proven. If you have blackjack and the dealer has an Ace up card the mathematical odds are 4 to 1 that he will have a 10 value card underneath. These are pretty good odds in your favor which is why the casino wants you to take insurance. The same mathematical formula goes with having two 8's. The percentages show that you will win one of these hands by splitting the 8's versus hitting that hard 16. Dollar wise you will be way ahead by following these rules. Being perfect in basic strategy still gives the house a 51% to 49% edge on you, a 2% difference in their favor. While knowing basic strategy still gives the house a 2% edge on you, not knowing basic strategy increases the house's odds of winning 15%-20%. So you ask yourself, "If the casino has a 2% edge on me how can I win?" Good question, I'll cover this in detail in Rule #3, coming up next.

Rule #3 / // /// //// *MONEY MANAGEMENT*

You cannot win consistently at blackjack without being perfect at all five rules, however, if I were to pick only one as being the most important it would be money management. It is also the most disagreed upon by the experts in the field. You can have the proper bankroll, be perfect in basic strategy, know the trends, have great discipline and still not be a consistent winner. You ask yourself why not? The answer is: if you don't know how to manage your money you won't have any to manage.

Managing money is one of the hardest things to do not only in blackjack but in everyday life. How many times have you heard about people who have won millions of dollars in the lottery only to be broke and in debt a year later? The reason is bad money management. Let me hit closer to home, how many times have you been lucky enough to have won a large amount of money at a casino and a week later have nothing to show for it? I use the word lucky because up until now you have exhibited no skill, only luck. Unfortunately you can't win consistently in a casino without a formula. That is why I am giving you a way to win consistently with proven mathematical percentages that are in your favor not the casinos.

Financial planners make a lot of money managing other peoples money, now I'm going to give you an easy system of handling your own while playing blackjack. It is called the telephone number because this is what it resembles.

It begins like this, your first bet at every table must be twice the table minimum, for example, at a $5 table your first bet is $10. If you win, you regress your next bet to $5 because winning two hands in a row is very difficult. So by winning your first bet and losing your second you are ahead of the casino. Now, say you win your second bet, your third bet would increase by one unit (the table minimum) or, as in my example, to $10. Keep increasing your bet by one unit each time you win even if the dealer reshuffles and starts a new shoe. If you push or tie the dealer use the same bet for the next hand. If you push again you should maintain the same bet until you either win or lose. If you win, increase your bet another unit. If you lose, immediately go back to your original bet, which would be $10. The exact same money management system is true of higher stake tables, for example, at a $25 table your first bet is $50. Now, here is the telephone number system I spoke of, based in units: 2-1-2-3-4-5, etc. An example of the telephone number system using a $5 table is:

1st bet: 2 units - $10, 2nd bet: 1 unit - $5, 3rd bet: 2 units - $10, 4th bet: 3 units - $15, 5th bet: 4 units - $20, 6th bet: 5 units - $25, etc.

This progression assumes you have won every hand, if at any time you lose you start again from the beginning of the telephone number.This money management system has the best chance of keeping you in the game until a winning trend develops. Trends are a mathematical fact, but if you have no money left the hottest trend or streak in the world won't help you. That is why money management is so very important.

I touched on the word trend. I will now go into detail as to why they are so important and how to use trends in your favor. This is such a powerful word that it becomes Rule #4 in winning consistently.

Trends have many names. They can be called streaks, trends or rhythms—they all mean the same thing. The best example I can give you of a trend is this—you have 500 pennies and you flip each one, by the time you get to your last penny you will have flipped about 250 heads and about 250 tails. However, if you mark them on a graph as you go, you will see that many times you flipped six or seven tails in a row and six or seven heads in a row—this is a trend. Stock brokers and financial planners consistently use trends to describe the stock market and other finances that their clients are involved in. Because you are my client and the trends in the stock market are no different than that of blackjack I now want you to pay close attention to what I am about to say. Before you sit down at a blackjack table I want you to observe the trends taking place at that table. This involves watching at least five hands to determine whether the dealer is in a bad trend, a neutral trend or just plain hot. You do this by observing the dealer's up card. If the dealer's up card is a 2, 3, 4, 5 or 6 he is having a bad trend. If his up card is a 7 or 8 he is in a neutral trend and if his up card is a 9, a 10 value card or an Ace the dealer is in a hot trend. The last thing in the world you want to do is to play at a table with a hot dealer whose trend might not change until you are out of money. The only time you sit at a blackjack table is when the dealer deals three out of five hands with his up card being a 2, 3, 4, 5 or 6. This could happen at any time throughout a shoe. You don't necessarily have to stop observing a table if you see a bad trend, trends change and a good one could be right around the corner. You just won't sit down until you see the trend change in your favor.

Now you might say to me, "What happens if the dealer's up card is a 2, 3, 4, 5 or 6 but when he hits he winds up with 21?" That's a good question, and the answer is that you can only base your decision on his up card because the mathematical percentage of his losing with those cards is dramatically in your favor. Just as the mathematical percentage of him winning with a 9 or 10 value card or an Ace is weighted heavily in his favor. Following the 2, 3, 4, 5 or 6 rule certainly is not a perfect science, but it does give you a proven mathematical edge over the casino.

There are other ways to decide whether a table is hot or cold, however none is as sound as the one previously stated. For example, my girlfriend goes to each table within the limit I am playing and outright asks the dealer if he's hot or cold. Usually the dealer will tell you the truth simply because you asked. I've heard dealers say "stay away tonight, I'm unbeatable" or "sit down I'm doing nothing but giving away money." Another way is to look at a table and see if there are a lot of chips in front of the players, this is usually an indication that they're winning. Neither of these two examples are scientific. I'm not saying that you shouldn't ask the dealer how they're doing or observe how many chips there are by the players at the table, both are good indicators, but I want you to base your decision on the dealer's up card and use the other examples as indicators and nothing more than that.

Let me speak of another type of trend. It's the trend that begins taking your money. In other words if you have just lost four hands in a row, leave that table whether it's a new shoe or the middle of an old one. Even if you have been winning at that table the trend has changed in favor of the house—remember what I said about playing against a hot dealer. You're not there to prove anything to anyone, you're there to make money only. Consider this a business, not a social event or a form of entertainment. Remember, even a happy loser is still a loser. Now it's time to talk about the last, but certainly not the least, important rule of my formula.

Rule #5   / // /// //// *DISCIPLINE*

Discipline is the emotional phase of my formula and by far the most difficult to learn. You can bring the correct bankroll, learn the basic strategy perfectly, correctly use the money management system and make the proper decisions on trends as they develop, however, without discipline you cannot become a consistent winner. Discipline, in my theory, is the unwavering ability to follow the above stated rules to perfection without giving in to emotions. Because discipline deals with emotion it's difficult to teach someone how to feel, it's not mathematical or scientific, much of it is plain common sense. You know your goal is to walk out of the casino a winner, and if you follow my five rules you will have a percentage edge over the casino.

Example: you just drove three hours to get to the casino, you're there for 20 minutes and you have a tremendous hot streak—you have increased your money by 50%, which accomplishes your goal. You've done something that most people don't do, you WON—you must go home. This is where discipline comes in and most people don't have any. They would analyze their situation by saying "it took me three hours to get here, I only played 20 minutes, now I have to drive another three hours to get home, so why not stay and have some fun?". Well, if losing is fun, they're in for a blast because that's just what's going to happen. This is what I mean about emotions and about how difficult discipline is to learn. Obviously the correct thing to do is to go home and then have fun. You can't lose any money if you're not there to do so.

On the flip side, you just drove three hours, spent 20 minutes at the tables and didn't win a hand. Good discipline requires you to leave the casino and drive back home the three hours, even though you lost your bankroll. Your heart is probably telling you to stay, but your head knows this is all you will lose if you leave immediately.

By now you should be able to see why discipline is so difficult to learn. How many times have you stayed on a hard 16 with a dealer showing a picture card, knowing the correct move is to hit, but the last five cards that were dealt were small ones and you figure if you hit you'll break, so you stand and lose more times than not. You have just compromised your basic strategy. How about the time you had a hunch you would win the next hand so you bet four times the amount your money management system tells you to and you lose on a whim? Then there was the time you walked into a casino with $100 and sat at a $10 table feeling lucky and expected to win immediately and you lost just that quickly. How about losing four times in a row and figuring that the law of averages should have you win the next hand and you proceed to lose the next three? These are all discipline problems that never should have happened, especially when you knew the correct move to make. Discipline is without question the hardest rule to learn.

Remember casinos are a business, they are there for one reason and one reason only. Can you guess what that is? If you said to take your money your answer is correct. Now that we know why they are there ask yourself why you are there. If it's for fun and relaxation you are reading the wrong book. You must focus on winning and *winning only* while in the casino. Once you leave the casino a winner *your fun* begins, and with that comes relaxation and a sense of accomplishment that you can enjoy with *their money*.

There are many ways in which the casino will try to distract you from the cards you are playing. They will give you free drinks served by an attractive waitress wearing next to nothing, they will tell you you're a great player even though you're not, and even go as far as to offer you free, yes I said free, food and rooms if you just play a little longer. Don't let them do it, stick to the five rules I gave you. Remember it's their job to misdirect your focus from the cards you're playing.

I remember a situation in which a man was winning $500 at a $25 table, he asked for a food comp, the floor person checked his play and said, "I'll be right back with your comp." The floor person purposely made the man wait one half-hour until he returned with a comp worth $40. During the half hour the man kept playing, not only losing the $500 he had won but also $200 more of his own. That $40 comp cost him $700—the floor person was good at his job and succeeded in making a loser out of a winner. The man misfocused his discipline and the casino won. Remember Rule #1: when you reach your win goal, stop playing. If that man had stopped playing, colored in his chips and told the floor person, "I'm finished playing for now, I'll wait here until you bring me my comp," I guarantee that the comp would have arrived within five minutes. The floor person would have realized that the man was done playing for now, and that if he got some food hopefully he'd return later. The casinos have many ways to break down your discipline, and they are very good at it.

I also strongly suggest that you never drink alcohol either before or during your blackjack session—for obvious reasons. Personally, I drink coffee, it keeps me awake and focused. Remember, there are laws about driving a car while intoxicated, the same rule applies to blackjack, the two don't mix.

Finishing up on discipline, I will emphatically re-state that it is the most difficult of my five rules. Once you learn and practice your discipline of not making decisions based on emotion the casino odds automatically change in your favor.

In summation, my five rules of winning consistently in blackjack only work by learning and following ALL five rules. It's hard to beat the casino, they have a lot of weapons and they use them all. If you use the basic strategy I outlined in Rule #2, mathematical percentages, together with my money management system, Rule #3, you will have an edge over the casino. Combine those rules with Rules 1, 4 and 5 and you now have a powerful weapon that will put fear in any casino's eyes.

Remember the casino is your enemy not your friend, treat it as such. You know the story of David and Goliath: David beat Goliath because he used his weapon perfectly—these five rules are your weapon to bring the casino to its' knees. The results, being a consistent winner, will amaze you and will humble the casino, at least in the game of blackjack.

Remember, a theory is only a theory until it is proven a fact—until now a fact that I only shared with a few close friends. Mohammed Ali said, "When you say you can do something and you do it, you're not bragging you're simply stating a fact." This man is the greatest boxer who ever lived and I feel this is the greatest blackjack formula ever printed. The rest is up to you, ask yourself one question and one question only, "Do I want to be a consistent winner in the game of blackjack?"

I wish you good health and lots of wealth.

Blackjack Jargon

All professions have a jargon used in their occupation. Included here are terms found in this book (denoted in bold) along with others that all blackjack players should know.

Action   *the total dollar amount bet by the player on all hands played throughout a session.*

Bankroll or Bank   *the amount of gambling money the player brings to the casino.*

Bar   *to exclude a player from a casino or prevent him from playing blackjack or any other table game.*

Basic Strategy   *the optimum mathematical way for the blackjack player to play his hands.*

Bet   *the amount of money wagered.*

Betting Ratio   *the mathematical ratio between the highest and the lowest bets placed by a player.*

Black   *$100 chips (usually black in color)*

Blackjack   *an ace and ten-valued card dealt within the first two cards.*

Bop   *to jump from table to table as trends become favorable to the player.*

Break It Down   *to cut chips into countable portions or to separate them into colors.*

Burn   *the dealer's act of removing a card from play and placing it in the discard pile.*

Bust or Break   *to exceed a playing total of 21.*

Caddy Blackjack   *a private blackjack game where the deal rotates from player to player.*

Cage   *location of the casino cashier.*

Call Bet   *a bet made without money or chips, only allowed to players with excellent casino credit or with money in the cage.*

Chips   *the tokens used in place of money for wagering; sometimes called checks.*

Chunk   *to bet large amounts of money.*

Comp   *short for complimentary, the privilege of using casino hotel services free of charge or at a discount.*

Counter   *a player who counts cards to keep track of the cards played in order to determine whether the deck is favorable or unfavorable to the player.*

Cut   *the act of changing the order of the cards so the cards aren't stacked.*

Cutcard   *a card, usually a colored piece of plastic, which is inserted into a deck or shoe during the cut to determine where the next pack will be shuffled.*

Dealer *an employee of the casino who deals the cards, makes payoffs and sees the rules are followed at his table.*

Discipline *the unwavering ability to follow rules without giving in to emotions.*

Double Deck a blackjack game played with two decks of cards.

Double-Down a move that allows a player to double his bet after looking at his first two cards. He is then dealt one additional card.

Drop the total amount of cash plus the value of the markers drawn at a table.

Dumping Off when a cheating dealer gives house money to a player by over paying bets.

Early Surrender gives the player the opportunity to take back half his bet before the dealer checks to see whether he has blackjack.

Fill the act of bringing additional chips to the table to replenish the dealer's rack.

First Base the first seat on the dealers left hand side.

Five-Card Charlie a bonus popular in caddy blackjack were a five card total equal to or less than 21 pays the player 2-to-1.

Flash to show the dealer's face down card.

Flat Bet betting the same amount on each hand.

Floorman the pit personnel who supervises a casino table game.

Foreign Checks chips from another casino

Front-Loader a careless dealer who exposes his down card in the process of dealing.

Green $25 chips (usually green in color)

Griffin Agent an employee of the Griffin Detective Agency who is hired by several casinos to detect slot cheats, dishonest employees, and card counters.

Hard Hand *any hand that has the potential of putting you over 21 if you take another hit. Here an ace can only be counted as one.*

Heat actions or statements made by casino personnel that lead a player to believe he is suspected of being a counter or a cheat.

Hit to request another card from the dealer.

Head-On playing one on one with the dealer, the only player at the table. Also called head-up.

Hold the ratio between the amount won by the house and the drop.

Hole Card the dealer's bottom card dealt face down and not exposed until after all players have played their hands.

House Advantage the percentage favoring the casino in any game of chance, sometimes called the "vig."

Hustling   hinting or asking a player for a tip or gift (done by some dealers.)

Index   the number in the corner of a playing card which designates its denomination.

Insurance   a side bet which is allowed when a dealer has an ace up card. The player may wager up to half of his original bet that the dealer's hole card is a ten. If the dealer has blackjack, the house pays 2-to-1; if the dealer does not have blackjack, the player loses his side bet.

Joint Bank   when two or more players combine resources and play jointly off the total amount, sharing in the win or loss.

Leak   a dealer weakness, such as exposing a hole card or over paying the player.

Loader   a front-loader; a careless dealer who exposes the hole card in the process of dealing.

Loss Limit   the predetermined amount that the player is to lose during a session

Marker   a special casino check or draft used by the gambler to draw chips against his credit or money on deposit in the casino cage.

Mechanic   a cheating dealer; generally one who deals seconds.

Money Management   a system for manipulating money in order to make the best use of gambling trends.

Multiple Deck   a blackjack game played with two or more decks, usually four to six decks.

Natural   a blackjack or "snapper" that is an ace and any ten valued card.

Negative Swing   a period, usually extended, during which the player shows a loss.

Nickels $5 chips

Off-the-Top   at the beginning of a deck or shoe, immediately after the shuffle.

Pair Splitting   two cards of the same value or two ten-valued cards when they may be split.

Pat Hand   a hand totaling 17 through 21.

Pitboss   a casino official who supervises play at a group of gaming tables (referred to as a pit), often supervises the activities of several floormen.

Push   a tie or standoff in which the player neither wins nor loses.

Quarters $25 chips

Readable Dealer   a dealer whose hole card can be spotted by a player or another person in a casino.

Red $5 chips

Rubber Bands   *a system of assigning dealers to table games when the dealers are not assigned a specific table during their shift (so-called because a rubber band is often placed around a clip-board under the name of the last dealer assigned).*

Session   *a period of time played at a table where you either meet your win goal or loss limit.*

Shill   *a casino employee who plays to generate business for casino game; in Baccarat, called a starter.*

Shoe   *a container used to hold undealt cards, used when four or more decks are used.*

Short Shoe   *a pack of cards dealt from a shoe which is not composed of complete decks, usually 10's have been taken out (or 4's or 5's added) to the benefit of the cheating house.*

Silver   *silver dollars or $1 gaming tokens*

Sky   *an area above the main casino where play is observed through one-way mirrors. Also, the employee assigned to work in such an area; also called "eye-in-the-sky."*

Snapper   *a blackjack or natural*

Soft Hand   *a hand in which the ace can be counted as a one or an eleven or any hand where the next card dealt would not put you over 21.*

Split   *an option allowing the player to make two cards of identical value into two hands, betting an amount equal to the original wager on the second card.*

Spread   *to bet more than one hand, as "to spread to three hands of $500."*

Stand   *a player's decision not to draw additional cards.*

Steaming   *betting higher and higher, usually after a series of losing hands.*

Stiff   *a hand which has a small chance of winning, usually one totaling 12 through 16.*

Table Minimum   *the minimum wager permitted at a table game.*

Tapping Out   *to lose one's entire bankroll.*

Third Base   *the far left hand seat on the blackjack table. (Last player before the dealer.)*

Toke   *a tip to the dealer, or to other casino employees.*

Trends   *the tendencies of the cards*

Up Card   *the dealer's card which is exposed to the player.*

Win Goal   *the predetermined maximum amount of money the player is to win in one session.*

Wired   *to have a good hand, usually a 20.*

Personal Winnings Diary

Date	Casino	Time of Day	+Win or - Loss	Comments

Personal Winnings Diary

Date	Casino	Time of Day	+Win or - Loss	Comments

Personal Winnings Diary

Date	Casino	Time of Day	+Win or - Loss	Comments

Personal Winnings Diary

Date	Casino	Time of Day	+Win or - Loss	Comments

Rule #1 / // /// BANKROLL

You must have 40 times the table minimum.

Rule #2 / // /// BASIC STRATEGY

See front of this card.

Rule #3 / // /// MONEY MANAGEMENT

Formula guidelines: (telephone #) 2-1-2-3-4-5-6, etc.
In a push situation you stay with your same bet until you either win or lose.
   a. If you lose the push start the formula from the beginning.
   b. If you win continue to increase your bet based on the guidelines above.

Rule #4 / // /// TRENDS

Judge your decisions only on the dealer's up card. You must observe 3 out of 5 good hands before you sit down.
   Good hand: 2-3-4-5-6 (sit if 3 out of 5 good)
   Neutral hand: 7-8 (keep observing)
   Bad hand: 9-10 value cards or aces (leave table)
If you *lose* 4 hands in a row after sitting LEAVE that table, observe another.

Rule #5 / // /// DISCIPLINE

If you lose your bankroll *go home*, do not get more money from anywhere.
If you win 20 times the minimum table limit *go home*.

Email: MEnUMark@aol.com
World Wide Web: www.blackjacknocounting.com

Rule #1 / // /// BANKROLL

You must have 40 times the table minimum.

Rule #2 / // /// BASIC STRATEGY

See front of this card.

Rule #3 / // /// MONEY MANAGEMENT

Formula guidelines: (telephone #) 2-1-2-3-4-5-6, etc.
In a push situation you stay with your same bet until you either win or lose.
   a. If you lose the push start the formula from the beginning.
   b. If you win continue to increase your bet based on the guidelines above.

Rule #4 / // /// TRENDS

Judge your decisions only on the dealer's up card. You must observe 3 out of 5 good hands before you sit down.
   Good hand: 2-3-4-5-6 (sit if 3 out of 5 good)
   Neutral hand: 7-8 (keep observing)
   Bad hand: 9-10 value cards or aces (leave table)
If you *lose* 4 hands in a row after sitting LEAVE that table, observe another.

Rule #5 / // /// DISCIPLINE

If you lose your bankroll *go home*, do not get more money from anywhere.
If you win 20 times the minimum table limit *go home*.

Email: MEnUMark@aol.com
World Wide Web: www.blackjacknocounting.com

Copyright © 1999 by George Pappadopoulos

BASIC STRATEGY CHART   HIT = ⬜   STAND = S   DOUBLE = D   SPLIT = X

YOUR HAND	2	3	4	5	6	7	8	9	10	A
					DEALER'S UP CARD					
8										
9		D	D	D	D					
10	D	D	D	D	D	D	D	D		
11	D	D	D	D	D	D	D	D	D	
12			S	S	S					
13	S	S	S	S	S					
14	S	S	S	S	S					
15	S	S	S	S	S					
16	S	S	S	S	S					
A-2				D	D					
A-3				D	D					
A-4			D	D	D					
A-5			D	D	D					
A-6		D	D	D	D					
A-7	S	D	D	D	D	S	S			
A-8	S	S	S	S	S	S	S	S	S	S
A-9	S	S	S	S	S	S	S	S	S	S
A-A	X	X	X	X	X	X	X	X	X	X
2-2	X	X	X	X	X	X				
3-3	X	X	X	X	X	X				
4-4				X	X					
5-5	D	D	D	D	D	D	D	D		
6-6	X	X	X	X	X					
7-7	X	X	X	X	X	X				
8-8	X	X	X	X	X	X	X	X	X	X
9-9	X	X	X	X	X	S	X	X	S	S
YOUR HAND	2	3	4	5	6	7	8	9	10	A
					DEALER'S UP CARD					

BASIC STRATEGY CHART   HIT = ⬜   STAND = S   DOUBLE = D   SPLIT = X

YOUR HAND	2	3	4	5	6	7	8	9	10	A
					DEALER'S UP CARD					
8										
9		D	D	D	D					
10	D	D	D	D	D	D	D	D		
11	D	D	D	D	D	D	D	D	D	
12			S	S	S					
13	S	S	S	S	S					
14	S	S	S	S	S					
15	S	S	S	S	S					
16	S	S	S	S	S					
A-2				D	D					
A-3				D	D					
A-4			D	D	D					
A-5			D	D	D					
A-6		D	D	D	D					
A-7	S	D	D	D	D	S	S			
A-8	S	S	S	S	S	S	S	S	S	S
A-9	S	S	S	S	S	S	S	S	S	S
A-A	X	X	X	X	X	X	X	X	X	X
2-2	X	X	X	X	X	X				
3-3	X	X	X	X	X	X				
4-4				X	X					
5-5	D	D	D	D	D	D	D	D		
6-6	X	X	X	X	X					
7-7	X	X	X	X	X	X				
8-8	X	X	X	X	X	X	X	X	X	X
9-9	X	X	X	X	X	S	X	X	S	S
YOUR HAND	2	3	4	5	6	7	8	9	10	A
					DEALER'S UP CARD					

Order Form

Quantity	Description	Unit Price	Total
_____	Blackjack's Hidden Secrets	$11.95	_____
_____	Laminated Cheat Sheet	$2.00	_____

Other publications by George Pappadopoulos

Quantity	Description	Unit Price	Total
_____	Blackjack's Hidden Secrets II	$12.95	_____
_____	Surrender Rules Card	$2.00	_____

Shipping and Handling Charges

$4 per book (U.S. only), $1 per card (U.S. only). Contact us for other rates. UPS 2nd Day Air available for an additional $10 per shipping address.

Please allow 2 to 4 weeks for delivery.

Total amount for items _____

(NJ residents add 6% Sales Tax) _____

*Shipping and Handling _____

Total enclosed _____

Name _____

Address _____

City_____State_____ Zip _____

Daytime tel. # (_____) _____ (*in case we have a question about your order*)

Method of payment:

❏ Check or Money Order (U.S. Funds)   ❏ Visa   ❏ MC   ❏ Discover   ❏ American Express

Credit Card #_____ Exp. date_____

Name on Card_____

Authorized Signature_____

Credit card orders may include email address for order confirmation.

Mail form to:

ME-n-U Marketers

P.O. Box 127, Linwood, NJ 08221

phone 609-653-3069 or fax 609-653-8186